The Deception of Sorrow

By Jeffrey Allen Weyker

Table of Contents

To Olivia,

Thank you for walking with me through my final journey in writing. Thank you for embracing me and my words with your beautiful artistic vision. Thank you for coming into my life and reminding me of purity. And finally, thank you for looking to the heavens. I often wonder what you see. Know that I see the heavens in you.

With all the love in the world,

Jeff

What Lies Beyond Infinity

Everything is new and fresh. It's all a dream.

You're out of your flesh,

To view this love a whole with no seam.

The world makes sense and happiness is without measure.

There's no fear of any level of penance,

For with love, often, your pain is for pleasure.

What would you give for happiness? And what would you take for theirs?

How can this bliss last forever, no less?

As you now see the seam and all its tears.

Love can be confused. After all, it is its own being.

We don't understand its power or how it is used.

You love. That is the explanation with no meaning.

You did all you could. It can never be the same again.

You tried to push forward. But, in place, you stood.

Fear not, because your destiny awaits you around the bend.

Loss is always imminent. There's always an end to an inception.
Keep your hope intimate. This end is a deception.

Looking to the Heavens

I once said, "wouldn't it be nice if leaves could fall up?"

Likewise, wouldn't it be nice if they could just stay still?

Inside a portrait, rested a timeless girl,

Visualizing heaven in this colorful world.

I see the peace in each brush stroke,

Adhering to my words with a comforting cloak.

Too much of me is in a scope,

Hanging like a leaf with a fall to invoke.

Allotted by this tree was the tranquility it spoke,

Nesting in my brain like your paint had to soak.

Know I don't know you, nor what you see.

You gaze off the page in my memory.

Oh honey, don't you see the irony?

Urge yourself to look at your name's meaning and what it told me.

Freedom screams the perfect team.

Our hearts and minds intertwine and convene.

Raging arts no longer confined to the inclined modern means.

Your vision is of love and no matter what that girl has seen,

Ousts nothing, I see the world in her dreams.

Uniquely beautiful, is this girl sitting next to her tree.

3.

One Big Happy Family

Look how far we have come.

Like a baby, we began so pure and innocent.

A mother, father, two daughters and a son,

We loved and fought without hesitation or thought.

That is love.

We played and made work fun.

Without a care in the world, the kids lived freely.

We didn't know of what our parents knew, naturally.

The stress parents carry is just what they do, intentionally.

We were shielded by food, sleep and church bells.

That is family.

We do what we must for each other.

Even if it hurts.

That pain is love,

It was what kept us together.

That magical idea of family forever.

4.

Funeral

With another death comes another day.

I had to put my mask back on.

Your happiness is my sadness, these feelings we portray,

Are felt by billions when death is a just a pawn.

I'm going to be frank. My older sister died.

It's something I don't feel to be true,

But it is, just as when I knelt and cried.

I'm slowly losing myself. We went from three to two.

Girl did we fight, and boy did I lose.

They were nightmares I had always cherished.

Now, my dreams of you are back. I must recycle and re-use.

For there is no ore of us until I have perished.

We walk past the black dresses and coats of the mourning,

To sit down and stare at her urn.

It wasn't the words, but the cries that had torn me.

I have a new outlook before it's my turn.

5.

Mommy's Little Angel

My older sister's story is now done.

Her baby brother is now the oldest one.

Our fighting was always met with peace.

Her spot in our family is now my place to lease.

It was never a space I had wanted.

Being the first departed was what I had taunted.

So, I live for more, now with less.

I must be that pawn in this game of chess.

I think of her children, my lovely nieces.

Their lives are a puzzle of broken pieces.

They have the best parts of their mother,

All the more, for my mother to smother.

And so, the cycle spins.

A relationship repaired by her next of kin.

I, reluctantly, thank God for the dreams that loomed.

For our relationship's end was foretold and entombed.

My parents and I were blessed to have that closure put to rest.

But we are family, and we'll always carry and feel that pain in Ki.

6.

Bittersweet Agony

People are flawed, my sweet sister.

You were never meant to feel this pain.

I told you, if I could take your pain away, I would.

And Ki, I can't remove this permanent stain.

A part of me is missing.

I know you feel the same way.

Though, I'll never fully know the burden you carry,

I still share your love's array.

My eyes adjusted long ago.

I see in your darkness.

Our pains are different and even though I'm your brother,

I don't always know what is best.

Remember the days when we were children.

Remember she loved and will always love you.

Remember she is now free of pain.

Remember, most importantly, all feeling are true.

My eyes and heart do not betray me.

I see us together again. You, me, and Amy.

7.

Never to be Duplicated

In the shadow of billions, you won't find me.

I'm just that leaf on a tree.

I want to grow old and pave a way,

For the people old to celebrate my last day.

I have nothing to celebrate for.

My offerings and good deeds could be considered a chore.

Do I do them for my own satisfaction?

My and God's personal transaction.

In the end, there's no use for notoriety.

The same could be said for a sinner's "sobriety."

We leave behind people who knew us,

In hope to be remembered for being kind and courageous.

I don't need the world to remember me, just my family and friends.

I don't need them to forgive me, but to know I made amends.

My words are history and it's time to forget.

There will never be another me, never a duplicate.

8.

Accepting the Unacceptable

Why do we fall in love?

It transcends space and time, so it seems.

I understand the love for family and friends.

We instantly love family. We're each other.

We get to know and grow to love our friends.

So, what about love at first sight?

Is it a physical attraction?

Is your brain telling you to love out of spite?

You're all strangers but I still love you.

I still want to protect you.

I still want to know you and love you more,

So that I can fill all the photo albums,

Place all the trophies on shelves above my bed.

They're where they belong as they look down to me,

As I look up to them.

I feel like we're all deserving of love. It's almost a right to experience that unexplainable joy, often times, followed by unimaginable sorrow. We deserve to feel that too, so that we may appreciate the feeling in all its glory. And all its pain. A pain I gladly accept if it meant a loving memory.

Photo Album

As each page turns, my heart skips a beat.

It has never been so easy to travel through time,

To see sighs, cries, hellos, and goodbyes.

Moments in time to prove truths and lies.

By the bye, generation of love tell stories.

Some stories that remind us how gory love can be.

What it can create.

What love can become.

Are our futures influenced by pictures of the past?

We see the smiles and simply want them to last.

Sometimes they don't and that is ok,

Because the genuine moments are what should be on display.

We mostly smile with a face mask, for time.

Have we had it wrong all along?

Sixty years ago, photos were ballads,

As they sat with a frown with a broken bulb added.

As each page turns, I see pictures in motion.

Emotions can be endless like the views of oceans.

There's an end to these moments upon the horizon.

When the last slot is filled, and the smiling is done.

10.

Ki

Being one of the last faces I see before death,

It's fitting and poetic for you to be my last writing.

I've always had you as a place for comfort.

You're my perfect sighting.

My last living sister through blood.

You're my one true constant.

We can feel each other through distance like twins.

We share the same conscience.

You call me to vent and call me for advice.

Never assume you're a burden to me,

Because you go seventy while I go thirty.

I keep it "one hundred", I'm locked with my key.

Never change Ki and embrace the agony.

We're human and that is a bittersweet plague for me.

As I said before, we'll always be together, from the end to the inception.

Carry my love through sorrow's deception.

11.

A Little Star: Supernova

My love, this journey you started is coming to an end.

There's a reason why you represent the number eleven.

You've been that luminous stellar explosion.

You've comforted my ominous implosion.

Know how often I think of you.

You're surrounded by black, but I understand and feel blue.

Twinkle in the heavens, right where you belong.

My angel for me and others is what you've been all along.

Thank you for showing myself me.

Thank you for my poetry.

Thank you for giving me this chapter.

Thank you for being my love's captor.

What will be written is done and the future will be said.

The world will read what I dream in bed.

I love you. I love you from afar.

You'll always be my little star.

12.

Tattoo

You found the love you had always sought.

Now, here you are about to tie the knot.

You struck the lottery when you played a life slot.

A king in his own Camelot.

How can I thank you for introducing me to your beautiful bride?

A sweet friend whose light blinds eyes.

How can we thank you for two beautiful kids,

And their essence of innocence continued from you vintage lineage.

How can I thank you for giving my world a little star?

She gave me a new meaning to a love's avatar.

I'm grateful for your who family.

They have loved and accepted the man in me.

You listened to me cry when I was stargazing.

You made me feel alive when we were trailblazing.

I could never thank you enough for everything you do.

You're always a part of me as an ageless tattoo.

You changed my life and that is just what a best friend does.

I look forward to your future and remember who once w.a.s.

13.

A Balance to Question

I personally, have a few ink tattoos. Why? I like to remind myself of what I have loved most. Also, I like to remind myself of what has hurt me the most. Experiences and thoughts that give us harmony and pure dread. Why do we torture ourselves this way? Is the universe balancing itself? Without experiencing happiness, we can't know sadness? Without pain, we don't know pleasure? Yet, we still torture ourselves by these scars.

We're ok and content with it because people need to feel some level of emotion. Is that why we ask questions? Is that why I ask that question? We need to know more to feel more, perhaps. Maybe that's why we are so critical of ourselves. I mean, we are our own worst critics. Individually, we feel like we know ourselves more than anything or anyone. So, because we have unlimited access to ourselves, we feed on ourselves. We ask questions about ourselves. Most of us start with the most basic question. Who am I?

14.

Who I Am

I know who I am. The question is, how do you see me? What are your opinions and thoughts? Does it matter? In a sense.

What I need you to see in me, is not someone who is straight or gay. Not even someone who is male or female, even though I am male. I need to be seen differently. I need to continue to project love, not just for my neighbor's or even the world, but for myself.

Even though I know who I am, there's a subtle desperation for other people to know who I truly am. Do I care what people think of me? No. Do I care what people know of me? Absolutely.

How can I spread love and hope if people don't see that in me? So, I'll continue to be weird while trying to be funny. I'll continue to surprise and give magical moments and memories. I'll continue to love strangers and tell them how beautiful they are, so that they may see the beauty in me.

15.

Trophies

When I think of this being, who is myself,

I picture the trophies on my shelf.

Don't get me wrong, my accomplishments are important,

But to have them define me would be ignorant.

I can always change and be more.

I can speak louder with whispers than roars.

I need to be above the labels,

So that your memories of me become fables.

The trophies mark a time from the past,

When my happiest moments were enshrined to last.

But they're not just statues of gold,

They're pictures and memorabilia that defined my mold.

I have plenty of shelves with much more space.

Will my future be a treat to taste?

See me. Accept me. Love me as an unlabeled one,

And join me on my shelves as another trophy won.

16.

Lord Jesus

I keep telling myself it's just the actions of a few.

What we know now, they already knew.

What's new?

I support Black Lives Matter and my police.

I understand the use of force but also peace.

Why can't we cease?

There is so much hate here.

The world looks at us and doesn't see strength, but fear.

And here we are in tears.

We're dying, separated by color.

Greene said he was scared and that he was your brother.

Think of your mother.

What can we do?

We're told to pick a color between black and blue.

It's a coup.

And we know it.

We choose politics over our hearts and disregard what fits.

It's a bit.

I can't let it be. I don't understand how you can't see.

Even after George died before pleading, he couldn't breathe.

I'm on my knees.

I'm praying so hard for God to give us harmony,

Because we're all in so much pain and I can't deal with this harm in me.

I concede.

We bleed. They feed on the seeds we need to grow,

So that our children could grow to be old,

And not die because of a traffic violation.

"Oh Lord Jesus. Officer, I'm your brother, I'm scared." – Ronald Greene.

17.

Powerless

We have to come together. We have to unite. We've fallen apart amidst our own personal pandemic with no shot for a cure.

I feel powerless. What will it take for all the hate to go away? Maybe it never will. I just find it so hard to believe that politics can have so much power over our humanity. I'm talking about our own person humanity.

What can we do? What can I do? Act like I'm making a difference in the world by being kind to my neighbor? I'm hardly scratching the surface. It would take the whole world to make the difference we so desperately need.

We must come together and walk united. But it's starting to get colder outside. I need to take a walk. I need to think of the many faces I am unable to help while I am still here.

18.

A Brisk Walk

I walk amongst my peers, family, friends, and strangers. Imagine being so unsociable, yet so comfortable around so many people. I still feel cold and alone. But it's a warming cold.

I look at each face and see time. Time filled with love and loss. Triumphs and failures tailored for me and what will come to be.

I walk carefully and gracefully. Not because I don't want to bump into anyone, but because I don't want to offend anyone.

I mind my own business in this and other crowds. Even though it hurts, I sometimes prefer to be in my own head. To wonder where my place is as I walk through this graveyard.

19.

With Grace

When you read these words, don't be frightened.

Just know I'll be more useful when enlightened.

Allow me to explain.

When we first met, I knew this one was special.

A friendship and love that exceeds every threshold.

So many lovely tales.

I remember our talks of God, laughs and emails.

There will come a day when heaven has an open seat,

For me.

I've prayed for years now and probably have become a bother,

But I've been allowed to be a guardian angel for you and my God-daughter.

And even though we don't always see each other,

I still love you like a baby loves their mother.

Here is the reward for me.

I'll be right beside you on your day of matrimony.

I'll be with you in your happiest of times,

Like when you're having your own babies and their earliest of signs.

More importantly my darling.

I'll be with you in your saddest of times when you feel most alone.

You'll know I'm there holding you, crying with you, whispering, "I love you" in my deepest tone.

You'll never see me, but I'm right there always protecting you,

Until your final breath when I take your hand to start anew.

An old woman turned back to a young girl,

God's gift to humanity, you're that priceless pearl.

I'll take you to your family again and that'll be my final endeavor,

Love and laughter. We're all together forever.

20.

Ember

For now, I remain here.

I watch an angel sail away while I cry at her pier.

My eyes are filled with happy ears knowing her journey is clear.

I see so much of my past in her.

Although, I remember how fast my clear path became a blur.

But she's a different angel with her own power to deter.

That's another reason why I'd rather not have death come too soon,

And continue to treat reoccurring wounds.

As my darling is presented for the world to swoon.

So, I need to learn to be better at looking for dawn.

I need to remember my dear is still a fawn.

I just love her so much, she's the meaning of a swan.

And that's all she really needs to know and for me to remember.

Her fire is just beginning to burn as I'm one of her many undying embers.

21.

Reflection

Whether they are a dear, star or little angel, I can't help but give a sigh of relief when I see them go out of their way to give back to the world in the most loving of ways. Hope replenishes, given the state of our country and how divided we are.

We need that hope and love, regardless of how minor they are. Regardless of how old and young the angels are. A simple smile can still change our future's history.

Act in kindness. Help a lost heart. See through their blindness and show them an end can be a start. Be your own art. Embrace what is a part of our nature to let the apart depart.

That, in itself, is our art as humans.

22.

The Eyes on Her

With each batted eyelash, my heart skips a beat.

I see beauty evolve through your instructions,

Teaching self-worth and self-love with your self-less deeds.

I ask, do you ever sit and wonder of how you're so proud,

To simply know someone and what they do for the world?

This girl gently kisses away clouds.

We all wish to be beautiful, inside, and out.

We all are, but sometimes we need help to see.

You devote your time and love to be with us on this route.

As we look at your allure, we ask for a cure.

Sometimes it's even harder to see our own truths,

But love, you're that smokeless mirror.

Your eyes are on us and ours are on you.

Remind us we're beautiful.

Remind us of what we once knew.

23.

Next Generation

I once asked God to keep the pen,

Then pass me the crayon.

I didn't want to grow older,

I wanted to continue being Peter Pan.

I'm at the age where it's now or never.

To that idea, I'm scared to say bon voyage.

But if it meant having a daughter and find so much joy in simply doing her hair,

I wonder if that is a premonition or just a love's mirage.

Am I fit to sit?

Am I fully equipped?

Can they survive the trip?

One they are proud to admit.

I must maintain stability.

I must stay grounded.

I want to set aside humility,

While sanding sharp edges to rounded.

Where is my soulmate?

Where is my playmate?

24.

Borrowed Time

As each year goes by, I keep getting surprised by the lack of luck
for death and where my truths lie.

I try and try to live a life that thrives as I wait for the end and
leave behind my lives.

But I stay alive, and I don't know why my body grows old while
being blessed by the five.

Maybe I'm meant to watch more loved ones die before I walk
with Grace and Jay to protect family ties.

Is it vanity's eyes that see my sanity fly away with another
birthday?

I long to say goodbye.

I'm afraid my mind will die before my body.

25.

Do I Know You?

You look in the mirror and know not who you see.

I's ok. I know you in memory.

You wonder why you have visitors who treat you as such.

Little do you know; you have a grandmother's touch.

Do you wonder why we are so empathetic with you?

We remember you treated our coughs like a deadly flu.

Family will be strangers, an unfamiliar tree.

You taught me to be good and treat strangers as family.

It's odd that with your age, you live again as a child.

I wonder if you ever feel acceptance or denial.

In a way, I'm somewhat envious,

For you have no choice but to be credulous.

I find peace knowing one day you'll be free,

Of this awful disease's tyranny.

This is the beginning with no end,

And soon you'll remember me again.

26.

Me: At Face Value

Sometimes I don't even recognize myself.

All the faces and personalities stuck in one body.

My mirror is a kaleidoscope.

How unfortunately beautiful,

To relate with so many people.

Still, I can't just see me on the other side of a peephole.

It's complicating who I am.

I know who I try to be and who I want you to see as me.

There are so many pieces like I'm a boardgame, waiting to be played.

And my player is a hero with a victim to be saved.

Who's going to live and who's going to die?

Who will I see when I squint my eyes?

Or are all of these faces me?

Each would be a piece of my anatomy.

Sometimes, I think too much.

27.

Happiness in Failure

Give me the toughest challenges, the most impossible feats and I will happily fall short. I know I tried. Some people could make the argument that success defines the journey. Be that as it may, I'll push back. I believe the journey defines what is seen as success.

If I could take all my loved ones' problems and it killed me, I succeeded knowing my loved ones are free of pain. Granted, I'd be dead, but I'll go out knowing success isn't reflected by money or power. I believe it's reflected by happiness, satisfaction, and love.

This is a different and nonconventional take. I need to succeed even if it means failure for the sake of my loved ones' successes.

28.

Coley

I couldn't imagine seeing my babies and feeling so much pain.

To know their daddy's gone and the struggle to stay sane.

Their daddy and your love was gone too soon.

He watches birthdays from afar and sees deflated balloons.

Nothing and no one can fill this hole.

You feel robbed of what happiness stole.

The sounds of your tears hitting the floor do not go unheard.

I know loss of family and the promised tomorrows deterred.

That's why I think of you and your babies.

We fear more of the "what ifs" and "maybes".

But they still have their mommy and daddy will never leave,

All your hearts and the love they still receive.

To Coley.

You know he wants you to be strong.

And he knows your struggles and despair could be long.

Try to remember, he's not going anywhere.

He's waiting for you with eternity to share.

29.

Idols

Who do you glorify?

Who do you look up to when you're down?

When you have no voice, who gives you courage for sound?

You're bound to them, and you may not even know,

Who they are personally, yet you know them from head to toe.

Do they make you feel envy or spite?

Do they make you feel wrong is right?

Either way, you can't get enough.

It's an itch to scratch but you can't even seem to buff.

Isn't that love?

30.

Strangers' Love

Think of the power and influence these idols can have. You love them and they don't know you. Think of the responsibility they carry, holding fate and choices in their hands as if they're equals. Do we really choose to love them or was it all meant to be because of who they are and who we strive to be? Or we envy?

But it's not that simple.

We can worship people we love. Often, they don't know we exist. But we worship our family, friends, wife and husband because their influence and existence make us better people.

Whether they don't know we exist, or they know us through and through, we love them. We are them and they love us too.

31.

One Life for Mine

Every poem or writing written is another piece of me I can't call my own. Sometimes, I feel exposed. I feel vulnerable and open to criticism, welcoming judgement with open arms.

When writing, my mind has to take me back to places where calamity and dejection is remembered to be inhaled through the pollution. The atmospheres offer not growth and life but tears and heartache. That's why it hurts so much to visit, and I can't return. I'll take what I can from those places, once more, to give to you. So that I may let them go and hope you can relate with my sorrow and spark a light in your darkness.

Just one person is all I could hope to be healed. One life for mine.

There's Always Another Bullet

We see our loved ones as people we would die for. We would in more ways than one.

We picture our loved ones facing harm, for example, an intruder in your home with a gun. You leap in front of their bullet and hope they are out of bullets. What a proving way to go. Heroic. Epic.

We find ourselves loving so much that it's painful. Not the feeling of love itself, but the idea of love. I love you to the heavens and back. Do you love me just as much? Would you die for me> Willingly and happily?

We ask ourselves these types of questions and come to horrible conclusion we would never dream to think of. We learn the hard way, through neglect, lack of appreciation and mental and physical abuse. They see "red" and you see "black."

33.

Black

Death is never what I intended to seek,

A feeling that I pray is peace for me.

Now your abuse is covered but I can still see,

All the memories that make me plea for sleep.

I was never afraid of your love turning to ash,

Surrounded by my love under a burning halo.

Every night I wept, as you refused to stall,

Enjoying my sadness while my happiness is owed.

You never ruined my smile until "we" became "I."

Obscure love for me was the genesis of my pain.

Upholding my rights as a bird who once sang,

Revoked your love for me, my voice and my fight.

Love was never truly there when you first said "hi."

Opening my scars is a terminal drug.

Vivid are your goodbyes and every breath is a sigh.

Evolve. Find myself. Fight.

33.

White

PTSD doesn't just go away. It can stay, linger, and eat away the best parts of us. Opportunities are everywhere and some can be so discrete. Some people meet their soulmates casually through school and work. Soulmates are what they are. You'll find them because you're supposed to, even if they're simply walking past you on a sidewalk. Don't be afraid to speak with the one person you're never supposed to be afraid of speaking to.

Can you tell the grass is greener?

Weight of the scars lifted. Now your future is leaner.

He took your pride and stole your might.

You still have fight because in the black, you see the white light.

And there he could be, your knight in shining armor.

God plays many roles, even a farmer,

Planting these seeds to pick or grow.

Your free will is back like the times of old.

Before, you were stuck in what seemed like a bottomless pit.

Just your thoughts of being free made him sick.

Now you are free to run.

It's a given for many, yet a gift to some.

Take advantage of this gift and turn around,

Say anything, regardless of how it sounds.

They could be that white light, the one you saw and always wanted.

Keep your abuser in the past and leave him there haunted.

35.

Heart

How lucky am I to be Irish.

Well, that comes naturally in a sense.

I'm proud of where I come from.

I'm Irish turned American.

Best of both worlds.

I'm red, white, blue, and green swirled.

Don't forget I'm from the Swedish Nightingale.

I have the ability to fly but I wait for Ki.

We're different but still the same.

We are Christians but never bail.

I'll be coming to my third home soon,

To sing, drink and tell them of the loon.

I'm accepted but still a loner.

May I still be fortunate as a four-leaf clover?

36.

Beautiful People

I see these beautiful people and wonder how we could share the same blood.

I know we're not all perfect, but your bridges are my mud.

Your soft tones are reflected in the male, but your tones sound different to me,

Accompanied by your smiles, your presences give me serenity.

I envy you because I always see you as having life together.

I think of how to be more like all of you and feel better.

Because I'm not, I'd still like to pretend I'm on your level.

I'm tired of fighting myself and the devil.

Know that I love and always think of you.

Holidays can never come too soon.

I wait for the food and the love we share,

At grandpa's house, where we think of each other in a circle of prayer.

37.

Gestures

We all know by now how much I love. The simplicity of love is what makes love so beautiful.

A smile. A wave. A hug can make my day.

When I receive these loving gestures, I like to project that back to the world.

Even on my worst days, when I tell myself I just don't want to be touched, an embrace brings tears.

Sometimes, we receive what we don't believe we need.

We do need love because we're human.

Give love to strangers.

Give love you to your neighbors.

Give love to your friends.

Give love to your family.

You never know how lost they are,

Waiting.

38.

The Wait

We're gifted life to watch our loved ones die.

It's a burden we carry, and I share your sigh.

I'll never truly know your pain, nor will you know mine,

But the loss of loves are the ties that bind.

A part of me is missing. I know you can relate.

Heaven is now more perfect for our future's sake.

We find comfort in knowing we will see them again,

For their home is the beginning with no end.

Though, we still cry. We still tithe.

We see them grounded, but remember love, they fly.

And one day we will too.

Passing on that grief for others to endure through.

The Wait will be remembered as we pray on our knees.

These feelings are ours to share, after all, we're family.

Don't be afraid to let your emotions unfurl,

Because I'll always be her baby brother, and you, his daddy's little girl.

39.

The End is Near

Writing has become too hard for me emotionally.

I feel more isolated as time passes.

That's one of a few reasons why I should stop.

I need to take a moment to speak to my readers.

Everything I write about is genuine and true.

Sometimes, I don't have the luxury to vent,

Which is why I've appreciated this chapter so much.

You read of my triumphs.

You read of my heart breaks.

All I ask is for empathy.

I just hope that I can help you be happy.

We all have chapters in life that come to an end.

This will be another for me.

These memories live on to be remembered forever,

By the people we touch.

It's healthy to listen to others.

Soon I need to listen to myself,

Because I've hurt myself for some time now.

I need to stop the bleeding.

Listen.

40.

In a Heartbeat

We're advised to love ourselves more than others.

I haven't been doing too good with that.

Though, I love myself very much, I haven't given myself enough attention and love.

I've been told that if I don't take care of myself, how can I take care of other people,

If I'm not here?

It's odd because I've always felt that I could do more if I wasn't here.

I work myself to death, not just so I can show people the world, but to be protected from my thoughts.

And my thoughts tell me all signs are pointing to an early grave.

Is it sick of me to say I wouldn't have it any other way?

I killed my body in my twenties making dollars with pennies.

I think of their memories.

In a heartbeat, I would do it all over again.

41.

Gaining Control

I've known many beautiful people but none more beautiful than those who shape me as a person.

Those who make me a better person

So, I've hurt my body for many years.

I neglected my body and ignored my ears.

You can be beaten with advice and yet nothing will register,

Until you see a story and see what's blessed in her.

She's a girl who fears sin.

Her smile makes you perk up and her work makes you perk in.

This is Sarah.

She's the teacher to my para.

Without even trying, she taught me to look at myself,

To take care of the beauty that is my health.

But is it too late?

Will I reap the whirlwind of my past mistake's fate?

If so, it's ok.

For I'm not the only one her influence has saved.

And there will be many more to come,

Long, long after my story is done.

42.

Cooley

You've always lifted me up, my carrier.

Together, we've broken racial barriers.

You're a role model and a lesson.

You're my best friend.

It's hard to comprehend,

How far we've come and now you're penned.

But you always have been.

There's not enough space to put all your text in.

I can't forget about "g" when I'm textin.

Sometimes, all we can do is text and call.

We always look forward to the next recall.

I love you, my brother.

My brother from another mother.

Ok that's just lazy writing. The dark knight deserves a better hit at bat.

It's an honor to be your robin and I'm going to hit this out of the park,

Because our friendship makes me rich and stark.

Ok. Even though I'm a poet, I'm not going to blow it because these words tie together but I still have to sow it, a little extra tight. I am robin but I still have the might to say these words for the dark knight who gives me light in the dark night.

There we go.

43.

To Spring from Their Offspring

I always miss my closest friends.

The further they go in life, the further they go from me.

I couldn't be happier to see them go.

Each step forward makes me that much prouder.

I'm proud to see them grow and succeed.

I live through my tattoo and Cooley.

They travel to my future as I remain in the present.

I could never imagine how sorrow could feel so pleasant.

I'll tough on that later.

This time around, my crutch is safer.

I get to see Tre and Jae grow.

I get to see Jay break the mold.

Children.

One way or another, I will see them grow old.

Whether I'm alive or dead, their stories will be told.

And they will grow old.

It will be a gift to take time and space then fold.

That is my future as I remain in the now.

My mind is the looper, taking a repetitive bow.

44.

Deserving

I feel this bliss.

It's like a strange, foreign kiss.

It's a welcomed feeling I somehow miss.

It's almost as if I deserved it.

To see a light still lit,

And never hear a tear drip.

It's still strange,

To not feel lost and psychotically deranged.

What a lovely change.

But my friends and their children are okay.

I've been balancing loss for decades.

It's time to watch these shadows fade.

45.

A New Life

All is right in my happy little life.

I'm loving this opportunity to breath and relax.

I take two steps forward and no steps back.

I'm free from the drama and have buried all the trauma.

With the world at my feet,

I seek my next feat and look forward to the streak.

Pain and aches are pieces of cake.

My new life is the future.

Goodbye to what I thought was sure because the new me is the cure.

I can now see what is ahead of me.

Sadness is blasphemy.

You can now see my back and the last of me.

46.

Losing Control

Maybe it is too late.

Years of self-abuse doesn't bode well for my body to last.

Is too easy to pass.

I'm one to always need to be in control of myself and what I do.

Yet, my needs are not met with the reality of the truth.

I'm losing more.

I'm getting more familiar with the floor.

I wake up to disgust from being pulled from both ends,

Of happiness and regret and what could have been.

I smoked and drank for more than a decade.

And now I reap that whirlwind, denying myself aid.

I've made my bed and will soon sleep in it.

I need to remember Sarah and the importance of staying fit.

I know my odds and I'll continue to defy.

If I happily fail, you'll know I tried.

47.

Dream Girl

I can't find peace in my dreams.

Amber was the last for me.

I experience nothing but horror,

And wake up wishing for her.

It's a continuous loop of desperation.

A reminder of my fear of meditation.

Sometimes I feel depressed,

Knowing being awake and asleep, harmony is suppressed.

A lot of my thoughts, when awake, are of dying,

Breaking me with the people crying.

But I try to stay strong with hopes to see Amber.

Years of this torture is a well-traveled meander.

I need sleep but I don't need the fright.

Loving to fly yet fearing the flight.

Oddly enough, I wake up when I die,

View sleep and death's tie.

Expect nothing and hope for the best.

I open my eyes as I lay down to rest..

48.

Remembrance

It was a beautiful life with beautiful people.

I couldn't have been mor happy to be sad.

It's a blessing some people don't understand,

Like when it feels good to be bad.

I pray for many reasons,

In case my death is near.

To have my love be forgotten,

Is my greatest fear.

I've loved all of you,

And have been in love with a few.

The tree's leaves fell,

With memories to spew.

And spew, the will,

Accompanied by embarrassed tears.

It put a smile on my face,

To give you a joyful rear.

In the end, these memories will fade with their visions.

To spread love and appreciate pain could be life's greatest omissions.

49.

Guardian

What will ripple from my death?

The relief of my debts?

Tears that are left?

I often wonder of the pain it will cause.

A pain to be paused?

You'd see what I saw.

I often ponder my impact in life.

Did I love with unsettled strife?

Did I spread love out of spite?

I often wonder if my memories will actually live on.

All along, the king was a pawn.

My sunset is your dawn.

I often wonder of the legacy I will leave.

Would I be naïve,

To doubt the protection Grace and Elliana would receive.

I wouldn't because I've known,

Of the promise and power of love God has shown,

Through us all.

50.

The Deception of Sorrow

Thank you for hearing my series of stories,

To conclude The Inception of Love.

Not all tales were hunky dory,

Given the title above.

There were happy moments and sadder times,

Then happy moments again.

These thoughts and memories of love are my rhymes.

Like time, love will bend.

Here's my point.

 Every beginning has an end,

And every end creates a beginning.

Sometimes, when we're holy, we don't foresee us sinning,

Because if we think we're not broken, how can we mend.

And sometimes we are broken, and the world no longer makes sense.

We can't write our futures when they're written in past tense.

Through all the darkness, is light in all its forms.

And the bind of your happiness and sorrow will be torn.

Take a leap. Take a breath.

The water's not so deep when you're facing death.

Always remember there can be happiness tomorrow.

And there lies the deception of Sorrow.

The End